Jesus Will Never Go Away!

A child's journey to find Jesus.

Written by:
Veronica G. Burnette

Illustrations by:
William D. Page
(at the age of 12)

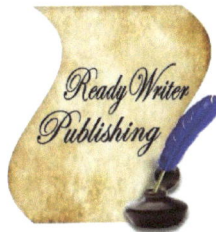

Jesus Will Never Go Away!

Unless otherwise indicated, all scriptural quotations are from The Holy Bible – King James Version.

Published by: Ready Writer Publishing
Durham, North Carolina

ISBN: 0-9743773-4-1

Veronica G. Burnette:
Workforce Development & Skills Trainer, Life Coach, Author & Motivational Extraordinaire
www.veronicaburnette.com

~ ~ ~ ~ ~ ~ ~ ~ ~

But Jesus called them unto him, and said

(Veronica's son Barryn at age 3)

Suffer the little children to come unto
me and forbid them not:
for of such is the kingdom of God

(Luke 18:16)

Mommy and Daddy took me to church today and I heard the preacher say

"There is someone who is always with you no matter where you go".

"His name is Jesus. He will be your friend forever and will never go away."

Wow! A friend forever, that
would be really neat.
This Jesus is someone I think
I would like to meet.

I asked mommy if I could be his friend too.

"Yes" She said. "He would love to meet you."

"Close your eyes and
ask him to come live
in your heart.

Once he is there he will never
depart."

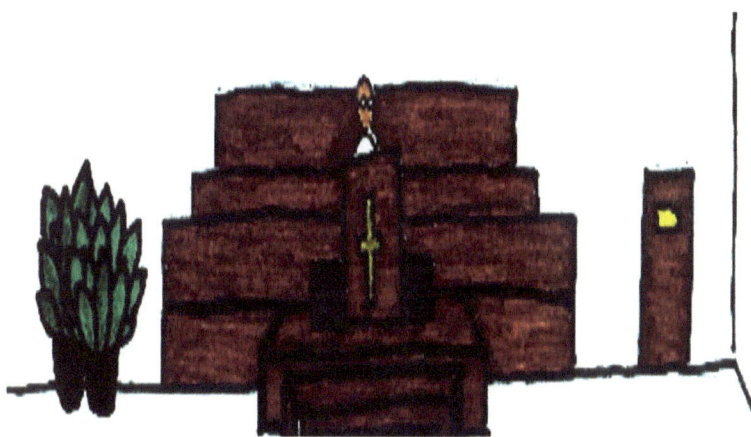

If he never goes away, then where can he be?

Mommy keeps telling me he's always with me.

So I looked and looked for him
high and low.

Where could he be?
Which way did he go?

I went to bed last night and said my prayers.

Daddy told me to give Jesus all of my cares.

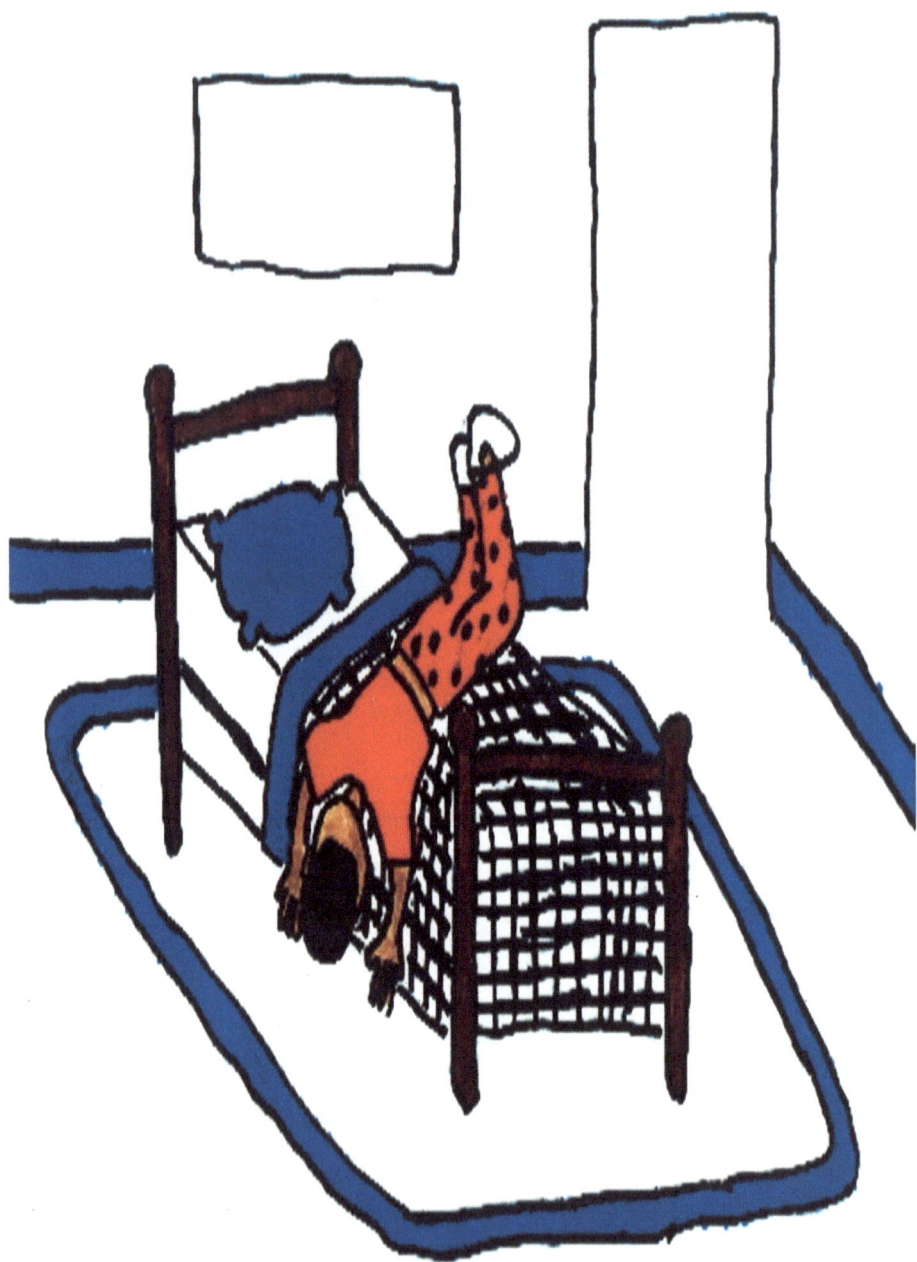

I woke up this morning looking for Jesus. He watches over me at night mommy says.

When I didn't see him, I looked on the floor. I thought maybe he had fallen out of bed.

On my way to school I thought "surely I will see him today".

We can eat lunch together and
at recess we can play".

When I went to the classroom
and looked for him there.

He can sit next to me,
I thought.
I'll save him a chair.

1 2 3 4 5 6 7 8 9

SCHOOL IS COOL

I looked around the room and everything was the same.

A new teacher walked in. "Hey that must be Jesus" I thought, until he told the class his name.

I just knew I would see him
because he is always around.

Where could he be? I know
maybe it's a game of
hide-and-go-seek and it's his
turn to be found.

So, I looked for him again and
again. I looked high and I
looked low.

Wow, he's really good at this game. Now where did he go?

I looked for him all day until it got dark and turned into night.

I decided to give up because he was nowhere to be found.

NOPE !
Not a Jesus in sight.

I told mommy and daddy that I was very sad.

They asked me how that could be with all the stuff I had.

"You told me Jesus would be with me always no matter what and wherever I go.

I can't find him anywhere. Can you tell me where he is because I don't know?"

Mommy looked at me with a
smile on her face.

"You see sweetie,
to find Jesus you only have to
look one place".

"He is in your heart
where he is never far.

That is where you'll always find
Him, no matter where you are."

You will never be alone.
You will always have a
friend no matter what your
do or where you go.

Jesus will be your best
friend forever!

What do you think Jesus looks like?
Draw a picture here.

Now draw a picture of yourself.

Dear Parents,

The world is a beautiful place when seen through the eyes of your child. They are a special gift from God. Remind them often how special they are to him. Your words become seed. What you plant inside of them will grow. Sow into them a harvest of good things. You will then watch them grow into the glorious creation God made them to be.

Abundant blessings!

www.ingramcontent.com/pod-product-compliance
Lightning Source LLC
Chambersburg PA
CBHW041802040426

42448CB00001B/17